W9-CIO-500

Stock Options

The Basic Investor's Library

Chelsea House Publishers

Stock Options

JEFFREY B. LITTLE

Paul A. Samuelson
Senior Editorial Consultant

CHELSEA HOUSE PUBLISHERS   New York   New Haven   Philadelphia

Marian Catholic High School
Chicago Heights, IL

DISCARDED

Chelsea House Publishers
Editor-in-Chief   Nancy Toff
Executive Editor   Remmel T. Nunn
Managing Editor   Karyn Gullen Browne
Copy Chief   Juliann Barbato
Picture Editor   Adrian G. Allen
Art Director   Giannella Garrett
Manufacturing Manager   Gerald Levine

The Basic Investor's Library
Senior Editor   Marjorie P. K. Weiser

Staff for **STOCK OPTIONS**
Assistant Editor   Karen Schimmel
Copyeditor   Terrance Dolan
Deputy Copy Chief   Ellen Scordato
Editorial Assistant   Tara P. Deal
Picture Researcher   Alan Gottlieb
Senior Designer   Laurie Jewell
Designer   Ghila Krajzman
Production Coordinator   Joseph Romano

Contributing Editor   Lee S. Cahn
Consulting Editor   Shawn Patrick Burke

Copyright © 1988 by Chelsea House Publishers, a division of Main Line Book
Co. All rights reserved. Printed and bound in the United States of America.

First Printing

1 3 5 7 9 8 6 4 2

Library of Congress Cataloging in Publication Data

Little, Jeffrey B.
  Stock options.

  (The Basic investor's library)
  Bibliography: p.
  Includes index.
  1. Put and call transactions.   I. Samuelson, Paul Anthony, 1915–
II. Title.   III. Series. HG6042.L57   1988   332.64'52   87-38224
ISBN 1-55546-628-1

CONTENTS

Learning the Tools of Investing

PAUL A. SAMUELSON

When asked why the great financial house of Morgan had been so successful, J. Pierpont Morgan replied, "Do you suppose that's because we take money seriously?"

Managing our personal finances is a serious business, and something we all must learn to do. We begin life dependent on someone else's income and capital. But after we become independent, it is a remorseless fact of nature that we must not only support ourselves for the present but must also start saving money for retirement. The best theory of saving that economists have is built upon this model of *life-cycle saving*: You must provide in the long years of prime working life for what modern medicine has lengthened to, potentially, decades of retirement. This life cycle model won a 1985 Nobel Prize for my MIT colleague Franco Modigliani, and it points up the need to learn the rudiments of personal finance.

Learning to acquire wealth, however, is only part of the story. We must also learn to avoid losing what we have acquired. There is an old saying that "life insurance is *sold*, not bought." The same goes for stocks and bonds. In each case, the broker is guaranteed a profit, whether or not the customer benefits from the transaction. Knowledge is the customer's only true ally in the world of finance. Some gullible victims have lost their lifetime savings to unscrupulous sales promoters. One chap buys the Brooklyn Bridge. Another believes a stranger who asserts that gold will quickly double in price, with no risk of a drop in value. Such "con" (confidence) rackets get written up in the newspapers and on the police blotters every day.

I am concerned, however, about something less dramatic than con artists; something that is not at all illegal, but that costs ordinary citizens a thousand times more than outright embezzlement or fraud. Consider two families, neighbors who could be found in any town. They started alike. Each worked equally hard, and had about the same income. But the Smiths have to make do with half of what the Joneses have in retirement income, for one simple reason: The Joneses followed prudent practice as savers and investors, while the Smiths tried to make a killing and constantly bought and sold stocks at high commissions.

The point is, it does matter to learn how financial markets work, and how you can participate in them to your best advantage. It is important to know the difference between *common* and *preferred* stocks, between *convertible* and *zero-coupon* bonds. It is not difficult to find out what *mutual funds* are, and to understand the difference between the successful Fund A, which charges no commission, or "load," and the equally successful Fund B, which does charge the buyer such a fee.

All investing involves risk. When I was a young assistant professor, I said primly to my great Harvard teacher, Joseph Schumpeter: "We should speculate only with money we can afford to lose." He gently corrected me: "Paul, there is no such money. Besides, a speculator is merely an investor who has lost." Did Schumpeter exaggerate? Of course he did, but in the good cause of establishing the basic point of financial management: Good past performance is no guarantee of the future.

That is why *diversification* is the golden rule. "Don't put all your eggs in one basket. And watch all those baskets!" However, diversification does not mean throwing random darts at the financial pages of the newspaper to choose the best stocks in which to invest. The most diversified strategy of all would be to invest in a portfolio containing all the stocks in the comprehensive Standard & Poor's 500 Stock Index. But rather than throw random darts at the financial pages to pick out a few stocks, why not throw a large bath towel at the newspaper instead? Buy a bit of everything in proportion to its value in the larger world: Buy more General Motors than Ford, because GM is the bigger company; buy General Electric as well as GM because the auto industry is just one of many industries. That is called being an *index investor*. Index investing makes sense because 70 out of 100 investors who try to do better than the Standard & Poor's 500, the sober record shows, do worse over a 30-year period.

Do not take my word for this. The second lesson in finance is to be skeptical of what writers and other experts say, and that includes being skeptical of professors of economics. So I wish readers *Bon voyage!* on their cruise to command the fundamentals of investing. On your mainship flag, replace the motto "Nothing ventured, nothing gained" with the Latin words *Caveat emptor*—Let the buyer beware.

Wall Street, New York City, in 1894.

Stock Options

S ince April 26, 1973, when options as we know them today were first traded on the Chicago Board Options Exchange (CBOE), the growth of the options market has been explosive.

The average daily volume on the CBOE that year was almost 10,000 contracts. Now, the sale of 70 times that number of contracts is not unusual. Overall dollar volume, based on the prices paid for options, has increased from $488 million in 1973 to billions of dollars today.

When options were suddenly "discovered" in 1973, they had actually been trading quietly for at least a hundred years. Some investment experts hailed them as a way to profit in any market—down or up—while others dismissed them abruptly as just another form of outright gambling. Professionals and investors who understand options, however, recognize that they are an additional investment tool and a means of managing risk for knowledgeable investors and seasoned speculators. This book discusses the mechanics of stock options and gives methods for valuing them and strategies for investing in them.

WHAT ARE OPTIONS?

An *option* is a contract under which one investor sells to another the right, but not the obligation, to buy (or sell) a specified amount of a particular security at a given price within a certain period of time. A stock-option contract is concerned with shares of specific stock, but it does not represent the purchase or sale of the actual stock shares. Buyers of stock options have the choice, or "option," of buying (or selling) the stock against which an option is written, but they are not obligated to do so. Whereas the purchase of actual shares of stock requires a large cash outlay, the purchase of an option on the same stock requires only a fraction of the cost of buying the stock itself.

Options are used in various ways to satisfy different investment needs. Investors can write options or buy options. The investor who creates an option is known as the *option writer* or *seller*. A writer sells the option to an investor who is the *option buyer*, also known as the *holder*.

Terms of an Options Contract

Most stock-option contracts have standardized terms. Each option is usually written against a hundred shares of the security being offered. All options contracts specify an ex-

ercise price and an expiration date. The *exercise price*, also called the *striking price* or, more commonly, the *strike price*, is the price at which an investor can buy (or sell) the optioned stock. This price is set when the contract is written and remains constant over the life of the option. The strike price is expressed in dollars per share of stock. For example, an "ABC 50" option refers to the right to buy (or sell) 100 shares of ABC Company stock at $50 a share.

The *expiration date* is the day the right to buy (or sell) the designated stock expires. If the option expires without being exercised (acted upon), the option is no longer effective. Most options are written for periods of one month, but they can also be written for three, six, or nine months. Whatever the duration of the exercise period, all standardized stock options expire on the Saturday immediately following the third Friday of the expiration month.

Types of Options

Depending on the type of option, the holder acquires the right to either sell or buy shares of a particular stock. A *put option* gives the holder the right to sell, or "put," a specific number of shares at a specific price (the strike price) to the option writer at any time during the exercise period. Conversely, a *call option* gives the holder the right to buy, or "call," a specific number of shares at a specific price from the option writer at any time during the exercise period.

Opening day, April 26, 1973, at the Chicago Board Options Exchange, the nation's first centralized exchange for buying and selling options.

For example, a holder who buys an "ABC 50 put" option may sell to the writer 100 shares of ABC stock at $50 a share at any time during the exercise period, regardless of the price at which the stock is currently selling in the open market. A holder who buys an "ABC 50 call" option may purchase from the writer 100 shares of ABC stock at $50 a share at any time during the exercise period, regardless of the stock's current market price.

This means that the writer or seller of a put option is required to buy the stock from a holder who decides to exercise the option; the writer or seller of a call option is required to sell the stock to a holder who decides to exercise the option.

Puts and calls are separate tools of investing and do not depend on each other. The purchase or sale of a put option does not involve a call, and vice versa. Each serves a different function within an investor's portfolio.

The Costs of Buying Options

For every option written, the writer receives a *premium* from the holder. The premium is a one-time payment for the rights conveyed by the option. The premium is retained by the writer and is not refunded even if the option expires without being exercised. It is, essentially, the cost of the option contract. Premiums are quoted in dollars per share of underlying stock. An option with a premium of $5 would have a total cost of $500 ($5 x 100 shares).

HOW OPTIONS ARE CREATED AND TRADED

Options exist only when sellers write them. If no sellers decide to write options against a particular security, then there will not be any contracts available for holders to buy. Sellers write options through their stockbrokers, who draw up the terms of the contract and handle transactions with other brokers representing options buyers. Brokers receive a commission or fee for each option transaction they handle.

It is not necessary for a buyer to exercise an option to make a profit on it. After the option is bought from the writer, the holder can trade it to another investor. The new buyer would pay a premium to the holder, who is now selling the option, but the original writer is still obligated by the terms of the option. The trading of options takes place in the *secondary market*.

Options on Other Securities

Although this book is concerned expressly with options on shares of stock, options are also available on other types of underlying securities. Investors can buy and sell options on U.S. Treasury bonds and notes, foreign currencies, and stock indexes. Indexes are a measure of the value of a group of stocks. Index options allow investors to speculate over a short-term period on the overall direction of the market.

THE HISTORY OF OPTIONS

The London Stock Exchange, where the organized trading of options on securities began, in the 19th century.

Options were first traded in the United States in the late 1700s, but they had been used in other parts of the world for centuries before that. The Greeks, the Phoenicians, and the Romans were all familiar with the concept of options. Options were also used on a widespread basis in Europe in the early 1600s. In the Netherlands the unchecked optioning of tulip bulbs led to the collapse of the market in 1636 and adversely affected the Dutch economy for many years after that. The organized trading of options on securities began in London later in the 17th century. Partly because of the speculative nature of options and partly because of their disastrous effect on Holland's economy, options were declared illegal in England in 1733. Nonetheless, trading on options continued in London, even though the law banning them was not repealed until 1860. Late in the 19th century the modern system of puts and calls was developed by American capitalist and financier Russell Sage (1816–1906), who devised the method as a means of circumventing laws pertaining to the lending of money.

By the 1920s most options activity in the United States was centered in New York City's financial district. Each day a small group of put-and-call brokers met in a restaurant on New Street. These options traders turned the place into their own office, as well as dining room and after-hours club. They arrived early and set up shop near the public telephone booths, their pockets jingling with change for the many calls they routinely made. Some of the more prosperous brokers employed messengers to traverse the Wall Street area in an attempt to bring buyers and sellers together. Matching a buyer and seller was usually difficult and often impossible. It required numerous telephone calls and exasperating negotiations between the two. Each option contract was written to unique specifications, setting forth the terms agreed upon by each buyer and seller. The broker's task was made even more difficult if the buyer or seller decided the contract was no longer useful. Because every contract was different, trading a previously written option at a profit was not easy.

Options were traded in this manner until 1973, when the CBOE began trading options with standardized terms. The CBOE grew out of the Chicago Board of Trade, where futures, options on wheat, soybeans, potatoes, and other commodities have been traded for many years. The trading floor of the CBOE was built in the airspace above the commodities exchange. After the establishment of the CBOE, other exchanges followed suit and began trading options with standardized terms. Today five exchanges trade stock options contracts: the CBOE, the American Stock Exchange, the New York Stock Exchange, the Philadelphia Stock Exchange, and the Pacific Stock Exchange. All are regulated by the Securities and Exchange Commission, the federal government agency that monitors the securities exchanges and the over-the-counter market for inequitable and unfair practices.

Today's Option Market

The standardization of the terms of an option contract by the CBOE in 1973 revolutionized the options market and made the large-scale trading of options feasible. Previously each option had been a separate and unique contract negotiated by special put-and-call brokers representing the buyer and seller. After April 1973, however, all options within a specific group had identical strike prices and expiration dates; only the premium had to be negotiated by representatives of the buyer and seller, which made the

The Chicago Board Options Exchange, largest of the five American exchanges on which options are traded.

Enthusiastic floor brokers crowd around a trading counter at the Pacific Stock Exchange. The floor brokers monitor trading activity closely and try to match buyers with sellers.

selling and trading of options much easier. Now buyers and sellers could select from among various contracts on the same underlying stock with each contract having the same specified terms but a different price, or premium.

At the time the CBOE introduced standardized options, it also established the Options Clearing Corporation (OCC). The OCC serves as a giant bookkeeping operation that processes all options transactions, not only original sales and purchases but also secondary trades. When a buyer exercises an option, the OCC assigns the exercise to a writer. The OCC also acts as a go-between for options buyers and sellers. After representatives of the buyer and the seller match an order to buy with an order to sell, the buyer and seller no longer have any direct contact. Instead, the OCC becomes the options buyer to every seller and the options seller to every buyer. The OCC guarantees settlement of all contracts: An option writer's obligations to perform according to the terms of the contract are with the OCC rather than to an individual buyer; similarly, the OCC is obligated to honor the terms of the contract to the option buyer.

The establishment of the OCC and the standardization of the terms of a contract have enhanced the trading of options. Standardized options are easily interchangeable; options with common expiration dates and strike prices can be substituted for each other. With standardized options, an option writer can be released from the obligations of the contract simply by buying an option equivalent to the terms of the contract that was written. Likewise, a holder who wants to terminate an option can simply sell it to another holder by instructing the broker to do so.

How Today's Options Market Works

Today's investors in options have a much larger universe from which to choose than had their predecessors. Not all stocks, however, can have options written against them. The OCC decides which companies' stocks will be available for optioning, primarily on the basis of the popularity of the underlying security. It also operates the lotteries that are used to determine which exchange will list, or carry, the stock option. Generally options that are listed on one exchange are not listed on another. Dual listing, the listing of an option on more than one exchange, does exist, but it has not been successful.

Of the five exchanges that trade options, the CBOE is the leader in the options market. There are 11 oval trading counters on the floor of the CBOE. The options of several underlying securities listed with the CBOE are traded at each counter. Outside the counters groups of *floor brokers*, representatives of individual investors or brokerage firms, try to match orders to buy with orders to sell. They listen closely for outcries of interest from other brokers and watch computer monitors that are above each counter for up-to-the-minute price information on trading activity. This information, which changes rapidly, includes the premium

The trading floor of the Chicago Board Options Exchange.

of the last trade, the current premium bid on the option, the premium price at which the option is currently being offered, and the underlying stock's trading information. When a premium has been agreed upon by both brokers, the results are quickly passed to CBOE employees stationed behind the counter, and shortly thereafter the new information appears on the screen above. Most of the information on the screen is also transmitted via electronic quotation machines to brokerage firms throughout the country. Representatives of these firms are stationed at communication booths that surround the trading floor. Clerks carry a client's order to buy or sell from a communication booth to the floor brokers, and they swiftly return to the booth with the completed trade information. The representatives in the communication booths then transmit the information to the client's broker at the brokerage firm. In this way, investors can quickly learn the results of a transaction.

INVESTING IN OPTIONS

Options can give investors additional flexibility in taking advantage of the ups and downs of the market. Investors in options are speculating that the price of the contract's underlying stock will or will not change. Because options are based on the anticipated movement of the stock market, they are not as stable as some other types of investments. However, for investors for whom safety is not the primary goal, options carry the chance of a large gain for a relatively small cash outlay and relatively limited financial risk.

Buying options and writing options are separate and distinct vehicles for investing. Each is used to satisfy different investment needs and each has its own risks and rewards.

Buying Options

Investors buy options because they offer *leverage*. Leverage is the ability to control a maximum of assets with a minimal cash outlay. In this way, buyers are able to spread funds over many more investments than would otherwise be possible. The holder of an option is able to benefit from any price change in the option's underlying stock without having to buy the stock itself, an investment that would require a substantial amount of money and incur large com-

CBOE files containing cards that hold brokers' orders. For a fee, brokers who are unable to match orders to buy or sell may place them with the CBOE.

mission costs. The cost to the buyer for this right is the premium, which is usually only a small fraction of the stock's actual cost. The options buyer hopes the price of the stock will move far enough and fast enough to offset the premium paid and produce a profit.

Options also offer buyers protection against a decline in the price of the underlying stock. Buyers who own the stock can purchase a put option on it. This gives the buyer the ability to lock into a price and sell the stock to the writer at that price even if the market value of the stock declines.

The risks involved in buying options are limited to the cost of the premium. If the underlying stock does not perform as anticipated and the option expires worthless, the most a buyer can lose is the total dollar amount of the premium. This contrasts with the investor who purchases the actual stock and who stands to lose a greater amount of money if the price of the stock declines.

Generally, most options buyers do not expect to exercise the option but hope to make a profit by trading it to another investor for more than they paid for it. The buyers of put options believe the price of the stock will go down soon. They hope to profit by trading the option or by selling the stock they own at an above-market price. The buyers of call options believe the price of the stock will go up in the short term. They hope to profit through the leverage they gain with options.

The following example illustrates how a buyer can profit on an option trade: In late April, an investor decides that the common stock of the ABC Company will increase in the next three months. The stock is currently selling for $40 a share. The investor could choose either to buy the stock outright or to buy a call on the stock. Because the purchase of the stock itself would require an immediate cash outlay of $4,000 ($40 × 100 shares), the investor decides to take advantage of the leverage that options offer. The investor purchases an ABC July 40 call for a premium of $4 ($400 for 100 shares). By late June, the stock's price has advanced to $46, a gain of 15 percent. The premium on similar ABC July 40 calls trading at that time has increased to $7, a 75 percent gain. An investor who trades the option now would make a profit of $3 per share (the difference between the premiums), for a total profit of $300. The actual dollar profit on the call option was less than if the investor had bought the stock itself in April and sold it in June, but the call option produced a greater profit as a percentage of capital invested.

If the investor had misjudged the stock's movement and it had declined rather than advanced, the maximum loss would be the option's premium of $400. The price of the stock could go down by more than the premium amount, but the buyer's loss would still be limited to $400. The option buyer might, however, be able to reduce this loss by trading the call to someone else and receiving a premium from the new buyer.

If, using the same example, an investor expected the stock's price to decline instead of increase the investor

BUYING ABC STOCK VERSUS BUYING AN ABC JULY 40 CALL OPTION							
	ABC STOCK				ABC CALL OPTION		
April	Bought	100 shares at $40	$4,000	Bought	1	July 40 Call at $4	$400
June	Sold	100 shares at $46	4,600	Sold	1	July 40 Call at $7	700
Trading Profit			$ 600	Trading Profit			$300
Profit as a Percentage of Capital Invested			15%	Profit as a Percentage of Capital Invested			75%

Brokers signaling bids at the Chicago Board Options Exchange.

would have purchased a put on the stock. Puts are calls turned upside down. They offer leverage and a limit on the loss of capital in a declining market. As the ABC stock declined, the premium of an ABC July 40 put would have increased in value. Purchasing a put also would have protected the buyer against a loss on the actual stock. The buyer could have sold the stock for $40 a share regardless of how much the stock's price declined.

Writing Options

Options sellers are known as "writers." This word has been used since the early days of over-the-counter trading, when the terms of each contract had to be carefully written out by hand. Although the terms of most options contracts written today are standardized, the word remains in use.

An option writer's primary goal is to earn additional income from premiums paid by buyers. Writing options is profitable only when the underlying stock neither increases nor decreases by more than the amount of the premium. The amount of profit a writer can earn is limited to the amount of the premium. The premium a writer receives is basically compensation for accepting the risk that the underlying stock could move adversely before the option expires and that the buyer could exercise the option at any time within the expiration period. If this happens, the writer will be obligated to buy or sell the stock.

For example, an investor who owns CDE Company stock currently selling at $50 a share writes a CDE September 50 call for a premium of $5—that is, $500 on the 100-share option. If the price of the underlying stock does not move before the option expires, the buyer will not exercise the option, and the entire $500 premium becomes profit. If the stock's price advances, however, the option may be exercised, and the writer would be forced to sell the stock at $50 a share. If the stock's price increases to more than $55 a share (the $50 strike price plus the $5 premium), the investor will lose money because the premium—the writer's profit—is less than the difference between the strike price and the stock's current market value. The writer will make a profit on the call only if the market price of the stock is less than the combined strike price and premium.

Premium income can also provide the writer with a cushion against a decline in the price of the underlying stock. The premium cancels out an adverse price change in the underlying stock in as much as the amount of the premium. For instance, if the price of CDE stock, selling at $50 a share in the example above, declines by more than $5 a share (the premium), the option writer will suffer a loss on the actual stock.

EVALUATING OPTIONS

I n evaluating an option's potential and choosing a contract that best suits their investment needs, buyers need to consider three factors. First, they must determine the direction of the underlying stock's probable price change: Will it go up or down?

Once the probable direction of the stock's price has been identified, investors must predict the amount of the expected move. This is necessary for the selection of the option's strike price.

For the buyer to realize a profit on the option, the stock's price must move favorably beyond the option's strike price by more than the amount of the premium.

A floor broker at the CBOE gets late trade information from a computer terminal at a communication booth.

The relationship of the stock's price to the strike price is the second factor options buyers must consider. This relationship determines whether an option has *intrinsic value*. Intrinsic value is the profit that would be made if the option were exercised. It is the difference between an option's strike price and the price of the underlying stock. An option that has intrinsic value is said to be *in the money*. Practically all options that are in the money will be exercised before they expire. The more in the money the option is, the greater the premium will be. A put that is in the money has a strike price that is higher than the current market value of the underlying stock. Because the strike price is higher than the stock's price, the buyer could make a profit by selling the stock to the option writer for more than its current price. Conversely, a call that is in the money has a strike price lower than the stock's current market price. The option has intrinsic value because the buyer could purchase the stock from the option writer for less than the current price.

For example, an EFG 60 call option on EFG stock currently selling at $65 a share would have an intrinsic value of $500 ($5 a share × 100). In effect, the buyer could exercise the option and purchase the stock from the writer for $6,000 ($60 × 100 shares), then resell it in the market for $6,500 ($65 × 100). If the buyer had paid a premium of, say, $250 for the option, the profit on the call would be almost double the capital invested (the $500 gain from the sale of the stock minus the $250 premium less the commission the broker receives for handling the transaction).

However, if the market value of EFG stock decreases to $60 a share, the EFG 60 call would no longer have any intrinsic value and would be said to be *at the money*. If the market value of the stock further declines to $55 a share, the EFG 60 call would cease to have any intrinsic value and would be said to be *out of the money* by $5 a share.

Intrinsic value is not a fixed measure. It depends on the current price of the underlying stock and changes as the stock's price changes.

The third factor essential to evaluating an option's potential is the time period within which the stock price will make its anticipated move. Because options are effective only for the period specified in the contract, buyers must accurately predict when a stock's price will move in order to profit from the option. In addition to intrinsic value, then, an option has *time value*. Time value is the amount of time remaining until an option expires. Options are a *wasting asset*: They lose value as time passes. Time value influences the amount that a buyer is willing to pay for the

INTRINSIC VALUE OF AN EFG 60 PUT OPTION AND AN EFG 60 CALL OPTION		
	EFG Puts at 60 Strike Price	*EFG Calls at 60 Strike Price*
In the money	Stock Price under 60	Stock Price over 60
At the money	Stock Price at 60	Stock Price at 60
Out of the money	Stock Price over 60	Stock Price under 60

option. An option buyer will pay a larger premium for an option with an expiration date further in the future because that leaves more time for a favorable change in the price of the underlying stock to occur.

For the buyer to realize a profit on the option, all three of these factors must be judged accurately. A failure to correctly predict one may lead to a loss of the entire investment, even if the other two had been judged correctly.

Setting the Value of Premiums

Premiums are set by the option writer but their cost is subject to negotiation between the buyer and seller. Each time the option is traded, however, a new premium is set by the holder, who is now selling the option. Premiums fluctuate depending on several factors: the price of the underlying stock, the amount of time remaining until expiration, the relationship or anticipated relationship between the option's strike price and the market price of the underlying stock, current interest rates, and supply and demand. These factors are used as a guide to setting the premium on an option and are not precise indicators. Usually, if they change then the premium will also change. Ultimately, however, an option's premium is set at the discretion of the option seller based on negotiation with the option buyer.

A floor broker at the Chicago Board Options Exchange holds slips that list price and order information for each client. These slips are passed on to a member of the CBOE when a trade is completed.

RISKS AND REWARDS

Nearly all forms of investing involve risks. But some types of investments are inherently more risky than others. Because the writing and buying of options is based on predicting the movement of the stock market, options are among the riskiest types of investments. There is significantly greater risk in writing an option, for example, than in buying a Treasury bill, whose principal and interest are guaranteed by the U.S. government. However, investors in options can adopt various strategies for minimizing and checking these risks and protecting the securities they already own.

The investment risks faced by options buyers are different from those faced by options writers. Buyers know exactly how much they can lose—the amount of the premium they must pay—but they cannot say exactly how much they might gain. Writers, on the other hand, know how much they can make—again, the amount of the premium, which they receive—but cannot know how much they might lose.

Every option has a mixture of risk and reward (profit). To come up with the best combination of risk and reward, buyers and sellers both must select a contract suitable to their investment needs from among the various strike prices and expiration dates available on the optioned stock. For buyers as well as writers, this will generally be an option whose strike price is slightly above or slightly below the current market price of the underlying stock. That is because the further up or down the stock's price is from the option's strike price, the more the price of the stock will have to move in a relatively short amount of time in order for the option investor to make a profit on the option.

A buyer's risks and rewards are the opposite of those of a writer. For buyers, options that have no intrinsic value (that are out of the money) offer greater risk but also greater reward. The further an option is out of the money, the less likely it is to move a sufficient amount in the allotted time for the buyer to make a profit on it. But if it does, the profits will be greater because premiums are lower the further out of the money the option is. Options that have intrinsic value (that are in the money) offer less risk and less reward. The further the option is in the money, the more likely it is that it will continue to have intrinsic value for the duration of the expiration period, and the buyer's risk is relatively low. However, the greater the intrinsic value is, the higher the premium will be. Thus, the option will cost more. In order to compensate for the higher premium, the stock must make greater moves in the right direction for the buyer to earn a profit on the option.

For options writers the more in the money the option is when it is written, the greater the risk and reward. The further the stock's price is from the option's strike price, the greater the intrinsic value of the option. And the greater the intrinsic value, the more likely it is that the buyer will exercise the option and the writer will be obligated to buy or sell the stock. If this happens, the writer will have to make up the difference between the stock's price and the option's strike price from the premium that was received when the option was written. Therefore, as the intrinsic value increases, the profit the writer earns on the option decreases. But because an in-the-money option commands a higher premium, the profit will be greater if the option expires without being exercised. The further out of the money an option is when written, the lower will be the risk and the reward. This is because such options are less likely to be exercised (so the writer has less risk of having to buy or sell the underlying stock); therefore, the premium the writer receives will be lower. Because there is less chance for the buyer to gain, writers lower the premiums they charge in order to attract buyers.

Managing Risk

Options can be used individually or combined in various ways to create strategies that balance a buyer's or writer's financial risk and reward. Both buyers and writers can make investments that effectively limit risk to underlying assets and decrease the potential for loss due to the speculative nature of options.

Covered and Uncovered Options   Investors can protect stock investments by using a strategy known as writing a *covered call*. An option is said to be covered if the writer actually owns the shares of stock against which the call option is written. The shares of stock are deposited in the option writer's brokerage account. When a covered option is exercised, the writer simply sells the shares of stock to the option buyer at the price specified in the option. The premium received when the writer sold the call will partially offset any loss if the price received for the stock is less than the call writer paid for it in the first place.

Writing covered calls is most profitable if the underlying stock does not move significantly up or down during the life of the option. For example, an investor who owns 100 shares of ABC stock currently selling at $100 a share writes a December 100 call for a premium of $7 a share. As long as the price of the stock is between $93 ($100 minus the $7 premium) and $107 ($100 plus the $7 premium), the writer will make a profit. If the stock's price falls below $93, the writer will suffer a loss from the decline in the value of the actual stock. If the stock's price rises, the option will most likely be exercised, and the writer will be forced to sell the stock at $100 a share. Any increase above $107 will be an out-of-pocket loss to the writer because the premium received will not be enough to offset the difference between the strike price and the stock's market price.

Not all options that are written, however, are covered. An option is said to be *uncovered*, or *naked*, if the writer does not own the shares of stock against which the option is written. Instead, the option writer deposits cash with a broker in a margin account. *Margin* is the cash or actual securities investors are required to deposit when a broker buys and holds stock in their account. The brokerage is, in effect, lending money to the investors to buy the stock. The margin serves as collateral (security) for their obligations to buy or sell the optioned stock. Individual brokerage firms set their own margin requirements, which must not be less than the minimum requirements established by the Federal Reserve Board and the stock exchanges. If an option is exercised, the writer of an uncovered option must be able to come up with enough money to purchase the underlying stock.

Because put writers buy rather than sell stock, put options are usually uncovered. The uncovered put writer will profit on an option only if the price of a stock does not

decline by more than the amount of the premium. The writer hopes to gain on the stock's decline by purchasing the stock for less than it is worth. For example, an investor writes an LMO February 80 put for a premium of $7 ($700). If the price of the LMO stock falls below $80 at any time during the exercise period, the put will most likely be exercised, and the writer will have to buy the stock for $8,000 ($80 × 100 shares). However, the real cost to the writer is $7,300 ($8,000 minus the $700 premium). Therefore, if the current market price of LMO stock is higher than $73 a share ($80 minus the $7 premium) but lower than $80 a share, the put writer will have bought the stock at a below-market price. However, if LMO stock falls below $73, the writer will have bought the stock at an above-market price and will suffer a loss on the put. If LMO stock is selling above $80 a share, the buyer will not exercise the option, and the total premium the writer receives will be profit.

If a put and a call have identical premiums, strike prices, and expiration dates, the uncovered put writer and the covered call writer will have identical risk and reward potentials. If a put option is exercised, the premium received by the uncovered put writer reduces the loss incurred by having to buy the stock. If a call option is exercised, the premium received by the covered call writer is added to any gain and may offset a loss incurred by selling the stock for less than the writer paid for it.

Some investors write uncovered calls. This is a very risky strategy that involves selling an option on stock that is not actually owned. Because the investor does not buy the underlying stock, there is no initial capital invested.

Therefore, the potential for profits is greater than if the stock were actually purchased. If the price of the stock either remains steady or declines, the option will expire without being exercised, and the premium the writer receives will be all profit. Because the stock is not owned, however, the writer of an uncovered call risks having to buy the underlying stock outright if the price of the stock advances and the call is exercised. If this happens, the uncovered call writer will be forced to buy the stock at the current market price, which would entail a large cash outlay. Every dollar the stock advances above the combined strike price and premium will be an out-of-pocket loss for the writer.

Hedging Options can be used as protection against an adverse move in the price of a stock owned by an investor. An investor can buy a put on the stock that is owned to act as a *hedge* against a decline in the price of the stock. If the price goes down, the value of the put will increase because the option gains intrinsic value. The buyer could trade the put for a higher premium than was paid, thus offsetting to some degree the loss on the value of the actual stock. The buyer could also choose to exercise the option, selling stock to the option writer at the put's strike price, which would be higher than the stock's market price. This would also produce a profit. If the price of the stock goes up rather than down, the put will be worthless and expire. The only loss to the buyer will be the cost of the premium. However, the buyer still benefits from the increased value of the underlying stock.

PER SHARE PROFIT ON EFG 40 CALL VARIABLE HEDGE					
Stock Price	Income from Premium	Profit (or Loss) on Stock Appreciation	Combined Profit on Premium and Stock Appreciation	Loss on 3 Calls	Total Profit (or Loss) on Variable Hedge
$38	$12	$ −2	$10	$ 0	$ 10
39	12	−1	11	0	11
40	12	0	12	0	12
41	12	1	13	3 (3×1)	10
42	12	2	14	6 (3×2)	8
43	12	3	15	9 (3×3)	6
44	12	4	16	12 (3×4)	4
45	12	5	17	15 (3×5)	2
46	12	6	18	18 (3×6)	0
47	12	7	19	21 (3×7)	−2
48	12	8	20	24 (3×8)	−4

Variable Hedging   Some options writers, eager to increase their premium income and decrease a potential loss on the stock they own, use a mix of covered and uncovered calls. This strategy is known as *variable hedging*. The variable hedger believes the price of the underlying security will go down and hopes to profit on the decline by writing more than one option against each 100 shares of stock. For example, an investor who owns 100 shares of EFG Company stock currently selling at $40 a share writes three EFG 40 calls for a premium of $4 ($400) each or a total premium income of $12 ($1,200). One of the calls is covered by the 100 shares of stock that are owned, and the other two are uncovered. The $12 premium would offset a decline in the price of the stock to $28 (the $40 strike price minus the $12 premium). However, if the stock advances, for each dollar above $46, the writer would suffer a loss of $2 per share. At $46, the $12 premium would offset the $6 increase per share of stock underlying each of the two uncovered calls.

There are, then, two points at which the writer of a variable hedge will neither profit nor lose on the combination of options. At any price between these two points, the variable hedger can make a profit. In the example above, the two points were $28 on the downside and $46 on the upside. For a variable hedger, every additional option written against the stock lowers the downside break-even point (so that the price of the stock could decline further before the writer will suffer a loss) but also lowers the upside break-even point (so that the writer will suffer a loss on an increase in the price of the stock at an earlier point). The writer will receive greater premium income for each option but will also face the substantial risk of writing uncovered calls. This risk, coupled with the difficulty of predicting short-term price changes in the underlying stock, makes the writing of uncovered calls difficult to justify as an investment strategy. Even if it appears certain that the stock price will collapse, writing uncovered calls is not the best method of profiting from an anticipated decline.

Puts and Calls Combined   Often unpredictable corporate or other events place investors in a precarious position. They know, or sense, that the price of a given stock is about to change substantially, but they do not know whether it will rise or fall. Such a situation might occur, for example, if a pending lawsuit is about to be resolved. If the company wins, the price of its stock might increase sharply, but if it loses, the stock price could drop just as dramatically.

In the interim, investors can protect their assets by employing a strategy known as a *straddle*. A straddle consists of an equal number of puts and calls purchased (or written) concurrently on the same underlying stock. All have identical strike prices and expiration dates.

Straddles enable options buyers to profit if there is a major price change in either direction on the underlying stock. But if the stock's price moves little in the option period, the potential loss to the buyer is limited to the total combined premiums paid. A significant price change up or down will be profitable because the buyer has the option of purchasing or selling the stock. Thus protected, the straddle buyer is relieved of predicting the direction the stock's price will move. However, the buyer must compensate by predicting the extent of the anticipated price change. Because a straddle usually produces a total loss on one side—either the put or the call—the price of the underlying stock must move sufficiently so that the gain on one side offsets the loss on the other.

There are two points at which the straddle buyer will break even, that is, neither gain nor lose. These points are computed by adding the total of the premiums paid on both the put and the call to the strike price of the call or subtracting it from the strike price of the put:

put cost + call cost + call strike price = break-even point A

put cost + call cost − put strike price = break-even point B

The Father of Puts and Calls

Russell Sage, American industrialist and financier, in 1903. Sage developed the modern system of put and call options.

One of the legendary figures of Wall Street was Russell Sage, called the "father of puts and calls" for developing the modern system of stock options. The son of an impoverished farmer, Sage amassed a fortune through his keen business sense, yet his miserliness and thrift were as well known as his financial exploits.

Sage was born in upstate New York in 1816, the youngest of seven children. Shortly after his 12th birthday he began work as a clerk in his brother's grocery store for $4 a month. He soon demonstrated that he had a head for figures and a knack for trading goods at a profit. By the time he was 13 he had enough money to buy some land—his first real estate—and by 15 he was successfully trading horses in New York City. He went on to provide financing for the construction of the nation's railroads, which was how he made his fortune and learned the fundamentals of business.

Sage was elected to Congress in 1852 and served as a representative until 1857. Shortly thereafter he brought his business acumen to Wall Street, where he increased his fortune by lending money at high interest rates. In 1869, he was arrested for violating state usury laws, which limited the amount of interest that lenders could charge. He was

B15048 ... New York, Nov 5 188 1

For Value Received, the Bearer may DELIVER ME OR CALL ON ME, on one day's notice except last day when notice is not required One hundred 100

Shares of the Stock of the Pacific Mail Steamship

Company, at Thirtynine 3 9 per cent., if Put, or at Fiftyfour 5 4 per cent., if Called, any time in ninety 90 days from date,

All dividends for which Transfer Books close during said time, go with the Stock.

Expires 1 1/2 o'clock, P. M. Russell Sage

A combination option written by Russell Sage for the right to either buy or sell 100 shares of stock in the Pacific Mail Steamship Company in 1881. Each option contract was negotiated between a buyer and seller.

found guilty, fined $250, and sentenced to five days in jail (which he never served).

Not to be deterred from profit making, Sage began dealing in options. With options he could charge high rates—in the form of premiums—without being subject to the usury laws. Although puts and calls had been used by professional traders and sophisticated investors for many years, through Sage they became available to the small investor. For only the cost of the premium, small investors could profit from price moves in major stock while Sage, as the writer, assumed the majority of the risk involved. To the unsuspecting buyer, Sage's puts and calls seemed a relatively inexpensive way to participate in the stock market. They probably would have been, except that Sage rigged the market on most of the stock options he wrote. He sold puts on stocks whose prices he knew would advance (and thus the puts would expire without being exercised) and calls on stocks whose prices he knew would decline. With this inside knowledge, Sage was able to pocket most of the hefty premiums he charged with little risk of having to make good on the options.

To protect his own stock holdings, Sage invented the straddle and the spread, two investment strategies that use a combination of puts and calls on the same underlying stock. As a result, he was dubbed "Old Straddle" by other Wall Streeters. He continued his profitable put and call business until his death in 1906.

Sage's business philosophy was "Any man can earn a dollar, but it takes a wise man to keep it." The "wise old owl of Wall Street," who wore secondhand suits and rode public transportation to work because he could ride free of charge (he was president of the transit company), Sage was worth approximately $70 million when he died. His widow, who inherited his estate, distributed much of the money to charities and foundations. Some of Russell Sage's closely hoarded fortune was used to establish Russell Sage College and the Russell Sage Foundation, which sponsors research to improve social and living conditions in the United States.

If the price of the underlying stock remains between the break-even points during the option period, the buyer will not profit by exercising either the put or the call options and so will suffer a loss.

Sellers who write straddles believe that the stock's price will change little, if at all. They are attracted by the substantial premium income straddles can produce if there is insignificant change in the stock's price. The straddle writer will profit if the stock's price remains between the straddle's two break-even points.

Creating a *spread* on the underlying stock helps to limit the risk of investing in options. A spread is the simultaneous purchase and sale of two puts (or two calls) on the same underlying stock at different expiration dates and or different strike prices. When a price change occurs in the underlying security, it generally does not have an identical effect on the value of the two puts (or two calls). This is because premium costs vary with the length of time until the option expires and the relationship between the stock's price and the option's strike price. The spread, therefore, changes as the intrinsic value and time value of the options change.

For example, an investor buys an XYZ October 50 call for $400 and simultaneously sells an XYZ October 60 call for $100 on XYZ stock that is currently selling at $54 a share. The spread between the two calls would be $300 (the $400 premium the buyer paid for the call minus the $100 premium he received for writing the call). If the price of XYZ stock advances to $60 before expiration, the investor would exercise the October 50 call, buying the stock at a per-share price of $50 (for a total cost of $5,000) and reselling it at $60 ($6,000). The transaction would produce a gain of $1,000 ($6,000 minus $5,000), against a premium cost of $400. In addition, the XYZ October 60 call would expire without being exercised, so the $100 premium the investor received for writing the call would be added to the profit on the spread. From an initial net premium cost of $300, the spread had widened to $1,000 to produce a net profit of $700.

Yet, if the price of XYZ stock advances above $60 a share, the investor's profit will not increase. This is because for every additional point above 60, the profit the investor might earn on the October 50 call would be offset by a loss on the October 60 call. For every spread, therefore, there are two points beyond which the spread cannot widen any further. If the stock price moves out of the spread range, the investor can no longer benefit from the strategy.

Puts and calls can be combined in several other ways to create investment strategies that have various proportions of risk and reward. In the *strip*, two puts and one call are bought (or sold). The *strap* entails buying (or selling) two calls and one put. These are complex investment strategies that are employed very rarely, usually only by sophisticated and experienced investors.

FOLLOWING OPTIONS: READING THE OPTIONS QUOTES

Information about trading activity in options is found in the financial pages of such major newspapers as the *Wall Street Journal* and the *New York Times*. Results of the previous day's activity are summarized for each of the five exchanges on which options are traded. The table presents price information for each class of options as well as the closing prices of the underlying stocks. A *class* is composed of all put options or all call

Workers at Pfizer Pharmaceuticals Inc. packing some of the company's products. Pfizer stock options are among those reported in listings in the financial pages of major newspapers.

options on the same underlying security. Thus, all Pfizer Pharmaceutical puts would constitute a class.

The excerpt on page 41 is from a typical options table. The left-most column of each entry lists the underlying stocks and the prices at which they closed on the previous trading day on the New York Stock Exchange, the American Stock Exchange, or in the over-the-counter market. Prices are quoted in points and fractions of a point. Each point is equal to $1. The fractions are eighths of a point, having a dollar value of 12½ cents. There are seven fractional points used in the quotation of stock prices: ⅛, ¼, ⅜, ½, ⅝, ¾, and ⅞. A share of stock listed at 30⅛ would

Trading in Stock Options

THURSDAY, DEC. 10, 1987

MOST ACTIVE OPTIONS

Chicago

Sales Last Chg. N.Y. Close

Calls

SP100 Dec230	20605	4⅞	—	2⅜	227.07
SP100 Dec240	20346	1⅜	—	1¼	227.07
SP100 Dec235	16634	3⅛	—	1⅜	227.07
SP100 Dec245	11542	13-16	—	13-16	227.07
SP100 Dec225	8424	8⅛	+	4⅞	227.07

Puts

SP100 Dec225	21964	5¼	+	2⅜	227.07
SP100 Dec220	21879	3⅜	+	1½	227.07
SP100 Dec230	14476	7⅛	+	2½	227.07
SP100 Dec215	12191	2⅜	+	1¼	227.07
		⅞	+	1½	227.07

American

Sales Last Chg. N.Y. Close

Calls

MMIdx Dec400	5987	2 15-16	—2	1-16	379.36
SFeSP Dec50	3535	¾	—	1-16	43⅞
MMIdx Dec395	3261	4¼	—	2½	379.36
MMIdx Dec390	2543	5⅝	—	3	379.36
MMIdx Dec410	2472	1 1-16	—1	1-16	379.36

Puts

BwnFer Dec30	2012	5	—	2⅜	24⅞
MMIdx Dec350	1676	2½	+	1	379.36
MMIdx Dec360	1604	3¾	+	1¾	379.36
MMIdx Dec380	1478	10	+	4	379.36

Philadelphia

Sales Last Chg. N.Y. Close

Calls

Clorox Dec25	723	2¼	—	⅛	26⅞
LomNF Dec20	600	½			16⅜
Placer Dec15	566	1⅜	+	⅛	16¼
Clorox Dec30	534	3-16	+	⅛	26⅞
G A F Jan45	475	.3	—	1⅜	44⅜

Puts

Clorox Dec25	701	3-16	+	1-16	26⅞
Textrn Dec30	442	9⅜	—	⅛	20
GS Idx Jan100	200	4	—	1	114.37
Waste Dec35	179	13-16	+	3-16	35¼

Pacific

Sales Last Chg. N.Y. Close

Calls

Compaq Dec50	1014	13-16	—	5-16	46½
Compaq Dec45	815	2⅜	—	¾	46½
Compaq Jan50	789	2 9-16	—	7-16	46½
A M D Jan10	754	¾	—	1-16	9⅛
Gentch Dec40	671	¼	—	⅛	35½

Puts

Micrsft Dec45	701	1½	+	1-16	47½
Compaq Dec45	636	1½	+	½	46½
EchoB Jan20	537	¾	—	⅛	23⅛
Gentch Dec35	470	1¼	+	7-16	35½

C B S 140

Total Call Vol. 261,695   Call Open Int.3,829,647
Total Put Vol.174,107   Put Open Int.1,163,015

American

Option & Strike NY Close Price	Calls-Last Dec	Jan	Feb	Puts-Last Dec	Jan	Feb
A M R 25	r	r	6	r	r	r
29⅜ 30		2⅜	r	1⅜	r	2¾
29⅜ 35	⅛	½	5¼	r	r	r
29⅜ 40	1-16	⅜	r	s	s	r
29⅜ 60	⅛	r	¼	s	s	r
A S A 40	12¼	11½	12¼	r	r	r
52⅝ 45	7⅜	8½	6⅞	⅛	1¼	2¼⅛
52⅝ 50	3⅜	5¼	6⅜	13-16	2⅜	3½
52⅝ 55	1	2⅞	4⅜	3½	5¾	6
52⅝ 60	¼	1½	2½	r	10¾	r
52⅝ 65	1-16	⅞	1½	r	13¾¼	r
52⅝ 70	r	s	3⅛	s	s	r
52⅝ 75	s	s	1½	s	s	r

Option & Strike NY Close Price	Calls-Last Dec	Jan	Mar	Puts-Last Dec	Jan	Mar
Alcan 20	r	5	7	r	s	r
25¼ 25	1	2⅜	3⅜	r	1⅜	r
12 15	r	r	3¼	r	r	r
PacGE 15	r	s	2	r	s	½
16⅝ 17½	⅛	7-16	1 1-16	r	1¼	r
16⅝ 20	1-16	⅛	¼	3⅜	r	r
Pfizer 40	s	3½	5	s	1	r
42⅜ 45	⅛	1½	2½	3	2¾	4¼
42⅜ 50	⅛	⅞	1⅞	7¾	7¾	r
42⅜ 55	1-16	½	r	r	r	r
42⅜ 60	1-16	⅜	r	s	18	r
42⅜ 70	1-16	⅛	r	s	r	r
42⅜ 75	1-16	s	r	s	r	r
Ph Mor 75	9⅝	10⅜	13¼	3-16	1	2⅞
88⅜ 80	4⅝	6¼	8	½	2⅛	r
88⅜ 85	1¼	3¾	7	2¾	4⅜	6¾
88⅜ 90	⅝	7½	2	4½	6	6¾
88⅜ 95	7-16	2	r	7⅞	r	r
88⅜ 100	3-16	s	1⅝	10⅛	10½	r
88⅜ 105	1-16	s	1⅛	s	s	r
88⅜ 110	1-16	s	1	19	s	r
88⅜ 115	1-16	r	r	r	25½	s 25½
88⅜ 120	s	s	⅜	r	s	s
88⅜ 130	s	s	⅝	r	s	r
88⅜ 135	s	s	⅛	s	r	r

Option & Strike NY Close Price	Calls-Last Dec	Jan	Apr	Puts-Last Dec	Jan	Apr
68½ 70	⅞	2¹¹⁄₁₆	5½	2¼	3¾	r
68½ 75	⅛	1¼	3½	r	6½	r
68½ 80	r	7-16	2⅜	r	r	r
68½ 85	r	¼	r	r	r	r
68½ 90	s	1-16	1⅝	s	r	r
68½ 100	s	1-16	⅜	s	r	r
Lotus 15	r	r	r	r	½	r
20 20	6⅜	7⅜	r	r	½	r
25½ 25	7½	2¾	4⅞	½	1¼	r
25½ 30	⅜	13⅛	2½	r	4¾	r
25½ 35	r	s	1¼	8½	r	8⅞
25½ 40	s	r	¾	r	r	r
Lypho 10	r	s	2¾	s	r	r
12½ 12½	r	½	1⅜	r	r	r
12½ 15	r	½	17⅛	r	r	r
12½ 17½	r	¼	r	r	r	r
12½ 20	r	1-16	⅞	r	7-16	r
ManHan 25	2	2	r	⅜	15⅛	2
26⅜ 30	⅛	½	r	r	9¾	r
26⅜ 35	r	⅛	r	r	14¾	14¾
26⅜ 40	r	¾	r	r	r	r
Masco 20	7¹⁄₁₆	2½	r	r	4⅝	4¾
21⅛ 25	r	¼	r	r	4⅝	4¾
Mattel 15	r	1½	3½	1	1	r
7¼ 5	r	10	r	r	½	r
7¼ 7½	r	¼	⅝	r	3¼	r
MenlGr 15	r	¼	⅛	s	r	r
18¼ 17½	r	1⅛	1⅜	r	r	r
18¼ 20	5-16	14⅝	1½1⅝	r	r	r

Option & Strike NY Close Price	Calls-Last Dec	Jan	Mar	Puts-Last Dec	Jan	Mar
43⅜ 40	r	r	s	½	1½	r
Seagle 10	4⅝	5⅛	5½	r	r	r
14¾ 12½	2½	2⅜	2¾	3⅜	⅛	9-16	1⁹⁄₁₆
14¾ 15	½	1⅛	1⅞	⅞	1⅜	2
14¾ 17½	⅛	s	1⅛	2⅞	3¼	r
14¾ 20	r	s	¾	6¾	s	r
14¾ 22½	r	r	½	s	r	r
14¾ 25	1-16	s	¼	10¼	s	10¼
SnapOn 30	4	r	r	s	½	r
33⅜ 35	⅜	r	2¼	r	r	r
Telex 40	1½	s	r	r	5-16	1
51⅞ 45	1½	9	r	¾	3⅛	3½
51⅞ 50	3½	5⅜	6¾	1¼	3	3¾
51⅞ 55	2	2½	3¼	3½	r	r
51⅞ 70	1-16	s	1⅜	r	s	r
51⅞ 75	r	5-16	1 1¹¹⁄₁₆	s	r	r
5⅜	r	s	½	r	r	2¼
Valero 7½	r	r	r	r	r	r
10 10	r	r	¼	r	r	r
49½ 50	⅞	2¼	3	1½	2	r
49½ 52½	r	⅜	1⅜	r	r	r
49½ 55	r	⅜	⅝	s	s	r
60 60	1½	s	½	¼	r	r
Firest 25	r	3¼	⅛	r	r	r

---

be selling at $30.125, 30¼ at $30.25, 30⅜ at $30.375, 30½ at $30.50, and so on.

The next column lists the various strike prices available for a class of options. When a stock's price has moved a great distance within a short period of time, there may be many options with different strike prices on the same underlying security. New strike prices are introduced by the various exchanges when the price of the underlying stock advances or declines beyond the strike prices available. This will usually occur at 5-point intervals.

The third column for an entry lists the expiration date and the premium at which a call option was last traded.

Floor brokers at the CBOE watch monitors showing the steady downward plunge of the Dow Jones stock average on October 19, 1987. The Dow dropped 508 points, an all-time record, on that day, and many options investors lost substantial amounts of money.

Most options are written for a period of one month. Originally, the expiration dates on options were three months apart. Options were randomly assigned January/April/July, February/May/August, or March/June/September expiration cycles. As shorter cycles became more popular among investors, the exchanges began offering monthly expiration dates on many options. The table on page 41 shows that options with expiration dates of December, January, and March are available on Pfizer stock. As each month expires, new contracts are introduced with expiration dates two months later. For example, as December expires, February will be introduced. The March expiration date is a carryover from the original three-month cycle.

Under the same heading, we see that the last trade for a Pfizer January 40 call took place at a premium of $3.50 per share. Because each option covers 100 shares of the underlying stock, the premium listed in the table must be multiplied by 100 to determine the actual dollar cost of a single option of any class. In this example, the premium would be $350.00 for one Pfizer January 40 call.

Sometimes, however, no options are available at an existing strike price under a given expiration date. This would be noted by a letter *s* in the tables. Thus, there are no Pfizer January 60 calls being offered. The letter *r*, as found under the Pfizer January 50 calls, means that options are available but that none traded that day.

The fourth column lists the expiration date and the premium at which puts last traded on the previous day. The meaning of the fractions and letters used in the call column also applies to the put column.

Premium prices on both calls and puts of less than $1 may appear in smaller fractions than eighths. For example, an option with a premium of ⅟₁₆ would be worth ⅟₁₆ of a dollar, or 6.25 cents a share.

HOW TO START INVESTING IN OPTIONS

Because of the complexity of stock options, beginners should consult a professional stockbroker before investing in them. Brokers can provide investors with general information, literature, and advice about options and the various strategies that can be employed with them. They can help tailor a portfolio to include a combination of investments that best suits the individual's financial needs.

GLOSSARY

"at the money" Refers to an option whose strike price is the same as the current price of the underlying stock. An option at the money has no intrinsic value.

brokerage, brokerage firm, or **investment firm** An organization that represents customers in buying and selling stocks and other types of investments.

call option A contract granting the holder the right to buy a given security at a specified price within a specified time period.

Chicago Board Options Exchange (CBOE) Established in 1973, the first exchange to trade standardized options; the nation's leading exchange in options activity.

class All put or call options written against the same underlying security.

collateral Valuable property used as security for a loan. If the borrower does not repay the loan, the collateral is forfeited to the lender.

covered call A call option for which the writer actually owns the underlying stock.

exercise price, striking price, or *strike price* The price at which an option buyer can buy (or sell) the underlying stock.

expiration date The last day on which an option buyer can exercise the option by buying (or selling) the underlying stock.

Federal Reserve Board The central banking system of the United States, which supervises the nation's banking system and sets appropriate monetary policy.

floor broker A person employed by a brokerage who carries out trading orders on the floor of a securities exchange.

hedge A strategy used by options investors to protect their holdings against an adverse move in the price of the underlying stock.

"in the money" Refers to an option with intrinsic value; either a put option whose strike price is greater than the current price of the underlying stock or a call option whose strike price is less than the current price of underlying stock.

intrinsic value The difference between an option's strike price and the current price of the underlying stock; the profit that would be made if the option were exercised.

leverage The use of borrowed money to magnify the potential gains from an investment.

margin account A brokerage account in which the client deposits a minimum amount to purchase securities, borrowing the remainder from the broker. In exchange for margin credit, the client pays interest to the broker.

option A contract giving the holder the right, but not the obligation, to buy (or sell) a specified security at a fixed price and for a fixed amount of time.

option buyer or *holder* The person who has bought an option contract and holds the right to exercise the option.

option writer or *seller* The person who sells an option contract and who is obligated to honor the terms of the option if it is exercised.

Options Clearing Corporation (OCC) The central clearinghouse, owned by the nation's options exchanges, that processes transactions and guarantees standardized options.

"out of the money" Refers to an option with no intrinsic value; either a put option whose strike price is less than the current price of the underlying stock or a call option whose strike price is greater than the underlying stock.

over-the-counter (OTC) market The nationwide network of brokers who handle transactions of stocks and bonds that are not listed on an exchange.

premium A one-time payment to the option seller for the rights contained in the option.

put option A contract granting the holder the right to sell a given security at a specified price within a specified time period.

risk/reward relationship The concept that investments of great potential return are likely to be less secure (have higher risk) than those with lower returns.

spread The simultaneous purchase and sale of two puts (or two calls) on the same underlying stock at different expiration dates and/or strike prices.

straddle The simultaneous purchase (or sale) of an equal number of puts and calls with identical expiration dates and strike prices.

strap The simultaneous purchase (or sale) of two calls and one put on the same underlying stock.

strip The simultaneous purchase (or sale) of two puts and one call on the same underlying stock.

time value The period of time remaining until an option expires.

uncovered call A call option for which the writer does not own the underlying stock.

underlying stock The stock on which an option contract is written, which the option buyer may purchase (or sell) at the price and within the time period specified in the option.

variable hedging A strategy in which the option writer uses a combination of covered and uncovered calls in order to increase profit and decrease losses.

wasting asset An asset, such as an option, that loses value as time passes.

FURTHER READING

Chicago Board Options Exchange. *Options Strategy Guide*. Chicago: Chicago Board Options Exchange, 1984. Provides basic information, evaluates various options strategies, and discusses the use of options for profit and protection in rising and declining markets. To order: Chicago Board Options Exchange, LaSalle at Van Buren, Chicago, IL 60605.

Levine, Sumner N., ed. *The 1987 Dow Jones-Irwin Business and Investment Almanac*. Homewood, IL: Dow Jones-Irwin, 1987. Includes a section describing options, futures, and commodities trading; also explains how to read options quotations.

Options Clearing Corporation. *Characteristics and Risks of Standardized Options*. Chicago: Options Clearing Corporation, 1987. Describes various types of options and the options markets. To order: The Options Clearing Corporation, #200 South Wacker Dr., 27th floor, Chicago, IL 60606.

Sarnoff, Paul. *Russell Sage: The Money King*. New York: Ivan Obolensky, 1965. A biography of the American financier and politician.

Teweles, Richard J., and Edward S. Bradley. *The Stock Market*. New York: Wiley, 1982. A thorough explanation of the stock market, including trading-floor practices, client-broker relationships, and much more.

INDEX

JEFFREY B. LITTLE, a finance graduate of New York University, began his Wall Street career in the early 1960s. He has worked as an accountant for a retail brokerage firm, as an instructor of technical analysis in a broker training center, as a securities analyst of technology stocks, and as a portfolio manager and advisory committee member for a major mutual fund. He is a Fellow of the Financial Analysts Federation, a member of the New York Society of Security Analysts, and was formerly a vice-president of an investment counsel firm in Baltimore.

PAUL A. SAMUELSON, senior editorial consultant, is Institute Professor Emeritus at the Massachusetts Institute of Technology. He is author (now coauthor) of the best-selling textbook *Economics*. He served as an adviser to President John F. Kennedy and in 1970 was the first American to win the Nobel Prize in economics.

SHAWN PATRICK BURKE, consulting editor, is a securities analyst with Standard & Poor's Corporation. He has been an internal consultant in industry as well as for a Wall Street investment firm, and he has extensive experience in computer-generated financial modeling and analysis.

LEE S. CAHN, contributing editor, is an investment executive with the Paine Webber Group. He previously worked at Merrill Lynch, Pierce, Fenner & Smith and is a graduate of Vanderbilt University.

PICTURE CREDITS The Bettmann Archive: pp. 8, 14; courtesy of The Chicago Board Options Exchange: pp. 15, 18, 19, 22, 26 (left); illustrations by David Garner: pp. 10, 11, 20, 26 (top), 28, 29, 30, 31, 32, 35; George Haling: cover; Steve Leonard/Black Star: p. 24; courtesy of the New York Historical Society: pp. 36, 37; copyright © 1987 by The New York Times Company. Reprinted by permission: p. 41; courtesy of The Pacific Stock Exchange: p. 16; courtesy of Pfizer Inc.: p. 40; UPI/Bettmann Newsphotos: pp. 12, 42.

19,771 ✓

19,771

DATE DUE

OC 14 '88			
19 '89			
MR 12 '92			
MR 22 '95			

332.64
LIT   Little, Jeffrey

Stock options

DISCARDED

Marian Catholic High School
Chicago Heights, IL

DEMCO